Van Gogh's
FLOWERS

JUDITH BUMPUS

❋

PHAIDON · OXFORD

To my parents, Robert and Mary Collison

Phaidon Press Limited, Musterlin House, Jordan Hill Road, Oxford, OX2 8DP

First published 1989
© Phaidon Press Limited 1989
Text © Judith Bumpus 1989

A CIP catalogue record for this book is available from the British Library

ISBN 0 7148 2585 9

Printed in West Germany by Mohndruck Graphische Betriebe GmbH, Gütersloh

Note
Van Gogh's letters quoted in this text have been taken from *The Complete Letters of Vincent
van Gogh*, 1958 (*see* p.80). They are all from the artist to his brother Theo unless stated
otherwise.

(*endpapers*) *Arums*. 1889. Pen, reed pen and brown ink, 31 × 41 cm (12^1/$_4$ × 16^1/$_8$ in).
National Museum Vincent van Gogh, Amsterdam, F1613 JH1703

(*half-title page*) 1 *Blossoming Almond Branch in a Glass*. 1888. Oil, 24 × 19 cm (9^1/$_2$ × 7^1/$_2$ in).
National Museum Vincent van Gogh, Amsterdam, F392 JH1361

(*title page*) 2 *Branches of an Almond Tree in Blossom* (detail). 1890. Oil, 73 × 92 cm
(28^3/$_4$ × 36^1/$_4$in).
National Museum Vincent van Gogh, Amsterdam, F671 JH1891

(*opposite*) 3 *Vase with Hollyhocks*. 1886. Oil, 94 × 51 cm (37 × 20^1/$_8$ in).
Kunsthaus, Zurich, F235 JH1136

(*pp.6-7*) 4 *Four Cut Sunflowers, One Upside Down*. 1887. Oil, 60 × 100 cm (23^5/$_8$ × 39^3/$_8$ in).
State Museum Kröller-Müller, Otterlo, F452 JH1330

CONTENTS

Van Gogh
&
the Great Book
of Nature

page nine

The Plates

page twenty-five

Further
Reading

page eighty

Index

page eighty

5 Paul Gauguin (1848-1903): *Van Gogh Painting Sunflowers*. 1888.
Oil, 73 × 92.5 cm (28³/₄ × 36¹/₂ in).
National Museum Vincent van Gogh, Amsterdam

Van Gogh

& THE GREAT BOOK OF NATURE

'A work of art is a corner of nature seen through a temperament.'
(ÉMILE ZOLA, *Mes Haines*, 1866)

Van Gogh's paintings of Provençal sunflowers, like blazing circles of energy and joy, will surely remain his most popular and inspiring images. He himself spoke of his special affinity with a flower whose rich colour typified the character of the South: 'that sulphur-yellow everywhere the sun lights'. His glorious paintings were emblematic of his gratitude for the happiness and serenity he found there. To his friend Paul Gauguin the sight of them was a revelation: 'That – it's – the flower,' van Gogh reported him as saying. These words must have rung as highest possible praise in van Gogh's ears; he had dedicated the whole of his short career to a study of nature, struggling to give it powerful and palpable expression. For today's audience it is Gauguin's portrait of him, at work on a vase of large sunflower heads placed beside his easel, that has come to epitomize this aspiration. As Gauguin imagined him, van Gogh sits rapt in his vision of the flowers. His gaze is fixed on the subject as, 'charged with electricity', he transmits it directly, almost instinctively, from eye through outstretched arm to canvas.

Van Gogh was proudly aware that he had revealed something new in his depiction of the sunflower: 'The sunflower is mine in a way,' he said. By sheer persistence of observation he had absorbed its nature so completely that he was able to render it unhesitatingly and with a freedom of interpretation that was entirely personal. The symbolic meaning attached to van Gogh's sunflowers has added to their appeal, but his paintings of irises, roses and almond blossom, among many others, show the same vigour of conception, and sparkle with similar freshness and conviction.

Many of his flower pictures were painted in series while the season for their blooming lasted and, as he related in the remarkably preserved correspondence he had with his younger brother, Theo, they provided him with colourful and ever-changing subject-matter: wild flowers among corn, flowering gardens and blossoming orchards, meadows of poppies and buttercups, branches of lilac, acacia, oleander and flowering chestnut. But for all their profusion, flowers were only one aspect of his love for nature in all her appearances, moods and weathers. Earth and sky, air, sun and stars, mountains, fields and trees, ears of wheat, dusty wayside thistles and blades of grass, farm animals, birds and nests, butterflies, moths and beetles were all, for him, part of the intrinsic beauty of creation, central to which was man.

Van Gogh's vision of the world was aroused at an early age, moulded partly by his highly sensitive awareness of nature, partly by his pious upbringing. He was born in 1853, the eldest son of a minister of the Dutch Reformed Church, and several of his images, notably those of the sower and the reaper in the cornfield and of olive orchards, alluded to biblical stories. Even after he had lost his faith in formal religion, his temperamental inclination to ecstasy lent fervent expression in his art to a sense that beauty was a quality both supranatural and eternal. 'You need a certain dose of inspiration, a ray from on high, that is not in ourselves, in order to do beautiful things,' he confided to Theo (Letter 625, February 1890).

According to one of his sisters, van Gogh loved flowers, birds and insects as a boy and impressed his family with competent copies of plants, flowers and wooded landscape. His first excited discoveries were made in the garden attached to his father's village parsonage in Zundert and in the countryside beyond. It was there, walking through the wheatfields, pines and heathland of Brabant, that he also became conscious of the calming and restorative power of nature. The impression of those childhood years touched him so deeply that some twenty years on, writing to Theo from hospital in Arles, he was able to recall the scene with utmost clarity: 'During my illness I saw again every room in the house at Zundert, every path, every plant in the garden, the views of the fields outside, the neighbours, the graveyard, the church, our kitchen garden at the back – down to a magpie's nest in a tall acacia in the graveyard.' (Letter 573, January 1889)

The mood of reminiscence spoke of something more than nostalgia for the past and for happier times. His strong desire to reclaim his roots in Brabant sprang from a vision, shared by contemporary realist painters, in which 'true civilization' was life lived in harmony with nature. In a letter to his parents, van Gogh wrote: 'In my opinion a simple farmer *who works, and works intelligently,* is *the* civilized man.... In the city one finds a few men who are almost as noble, though in quite a different way, among the very, very rare excellent people.... In general there is more chance of finding a reasonable human being in the country than in the city....the nearer one gets to the large cities, the further one gets into the darkness of degeneration and stupidity and wickedness.' (Letter 334, October 1883)

6 *Fourteen Sunflowers in a Vase.* 1888.
Oil, 93 × 73 cm (36⅝ × 28¾ in).
National Gallery, London, F454 JH1562

Anchoring his own emotional leanings in the theories and arguments of the day, van Gogh held that familiarity with a place was essential if man was to gain material as well as spiritual sustenance from his surroundings. The peasants were able to draw benefit because, by their very being, they already seemed a product of the land: '*They remind one of the earth*, sometimes they seem modelled in it,' he wrote (Letter 406, May 1885). In order to convey the reality of their lives, van Gogh felt that his activity must blend with theirs. He became a 'peasant-painter... ploughing on my canvas as they do in their fields' and painting 'with earth'. Through persistent hard work, in his dogged determination to teach himself to draw and paint, he mirrored their effort and toil. Describing his now famous picture of *The Potato Eaters* in 1885, he wrote to Theo: 'I have tried to emphasize that those people, eating their potatoes in the lamplight, have dug the earth with those very hands they put in the dish, and so it speaks of *manual labour*, and how they have honestly earned their food' (Letter 404, April 1885). He painted their skin tones with similar honesty '*the colour of a very dusty potato, unpeeled of course*' (Letter 405, May 1885).

In attempting to make a serious and truthful statement about a figure or about landscape van Gogh was conscious that his rendering of nature often fell so far short of the beauty he perceived in his subjects that it was bound to meet adverse criticism. But if *The Potato Eaters* is a harsh and ugly painting, there can be no doubt about the deep compassion expressed in it. To this extent he had satisfied the critical demand of the nineteenth century for the artist to interpret reality according to his own temperament. He had also met his own aim 'to progress so far that people will say of my work, He feels deeply, he feels tenderly – notwithstanding my so-called roughness, perhaps even because of it.' (Letter 218, July 1882)

The qualification expressed here by van Gogh referred to his uncouth appearance and unsociable behaviour, both of which pained his uncomprehending family. On another occasion he was provoked into a verbal caricature of himself as a big rough barking dog rushing clumsily round the room with wet paws. Beyond the obvious point that a warm heart could beat beneath an ungainly exterior, lay a conviction that an animal-like instinct to let sensations rip on the canvas without 'philosophizing' produced a more telling image. Although van Gogh prided himself on his modernity, this notion linked him, more closely than he might have been prepared to admit, with a romantic view of a primitive world in which peasants, animals, plants and children thrived in blissful innocence.

We catch a glimpse of his own attempts to preserve a state of artless simplicity when, as a young man of twenty in 1873, he visited London in the employ of the art dealers Goupil & Co. He was entranced by the beauty of the place: 'The country is beautiful here, quite different from Holland or Belgium' (Letter 9, 13 June 1873). 'In all parts of the town there are beautiful parks with a wealth of flowers such as I have never seen anywhere else' (Letter 9a to the Van Stockum-Haanebeek family, 2 July 1873). The freshness of vision could be kept continually alive to new sights, he believed, 'if only one has an open and simple eye'. As in Holland, he took long walks, enjoying the seasonal changes of flower and leaf, and he urged his brother Theo to do likewise.

But it is clear from what he wrote that his innocent eye on the world had already been tutored by art: 'Keep your love of nature, for that is the true way to learn to understand art more and more. Painters understand nature and love her and *teach us to see her*' (Letter 13, January 1874). His vision of landscape was essentially a poetic one, strongly coloured by his reading of John Keats and other Romantic poets, and elevated by a sense of beauty that suffused every experience, whether of life, art or literature. What he encountered in one area recalled its counterpart in another, complementing and reinforcing the sensation. The sky over the Thames brought a painting by Ruysdael or Constable to mind; a picture of Amsterdam by the Dutch artist Thijs Maris reminded him of Heine's lyric, *Meeresstille*. Moments of deep emotion so quickened his response to nature that the death of his landlady's thirteen-year-old daughter prompted a drawing of Streatham Common, sodden with rain. Increasingly, he was drawn to such atmospheric moments of 'still sadness', for nature both inspired and reflected feelings of romantic melancholia in him. The same romantic inclination was apparent in his preference for Gothic features, for the wild and irregular aspects of nature, such as moss growing over roofs, rampant ivy, gnarled and twisted trees. Of all times and seasons, autumn and the half-lit hours of dusk and daybreak were those at which he felt nature to be at her most 'serious and intimate'.

The painting that for him encapsulated these sentiments to perfection was J.-F. Millet's sombre picture *The Angelus*. This scene of a peasant couple praying in the fields at sunset possessed that mysterious and inspired quality which his mentor, the Dutch artist Anton Mauve, referred to as '*it* – that is beauty, that is poetry', van Gogh wrote from London in January 1874 (Letter 13).

As his mood crystallized into one of yearning for a less worldly life, he steeped himself in the teachings of the Bible and began to see things 'with a holier eye'. His social conscience and sympathy for the poor was strengthened by his reading of Dickens and George Eliot and of magazines such the *The Graphic*, the black and white illustrations of which depicted 'intimate modern life as it really is'. But the stirrings that finally persuaded him to renounce art dealing for a life of piety and self-sacrifice brought a shift of focus, rather than a radical change in his aesthetic persuasion. He wrote to Theo that 'a feeling, even a keen one, for the beauties of nature is not the same as a religious feeling, though I think these two stand in close relation to one another'. (Letter 38, 17 September 1875)

Some years later, bent on missionary work, van Gogh travelled to the Borinage, a mining district in southern Belgium, where he was appointed temporarily as an evangelist. There, far from the art world, nature alone offered him inspiration and the blackthorn hedges standing out starkly against the snow seemed to confirm his religious vocation 'like black characters on white paper – like pages of the Gospel' (Letter 127, 26 December 1878). But his excessive zeal in following Christ's example to the letter and his lack of eloquence as a preacher led to his dismissal. The sense of despair and loss of direction that for a time overwhelmed him eventually lifted. In the autumn of 1880 he rechannelled his urge to communicate into drawing, finding his first models in the peasant figures by Millet that he had admired earlier.

It was never van Gogh's intention simply to document. He made careful distinction between his studies, and he made literally hundreds in which he analysed what was in front of him. The final goal, the picture, was to be a distillation of thoughts arising from his subject and endowed with Mauve's 'it'. His robustly matter-of-fact insistence that the artist start from actuality,

& voici l'autre pièce de milieu des toiles de 22.

Terrain violet — dans le fond un mur avec des peupliers droits. et un ciel très-bleu

Le petit poirier a un tronc violet et des fleurs blanches un grand papillon jaune sur une des touffes à gauche dans le coin un petit jardin avec bordure de roseaux jaunes et des arbustes vertes & un parterre de fleurs. — Une maisonnette rose.

Voilà donc les détails de la décoration de vergers en fleur que je te destinais.

Seulement les 3 dernieres toiles n'existent qu'à un état provisoire *et devraient représenter un très grand verger avec bordure de cyprès & grands poiriers & pommiers*

Le pont de l'anglais pour toi marche bien et sera mieux que l'étude je pense

Suis bien pressé de retourner travailler. Pour le Guillaumin si cela est possible c'est surement bonne affaire d'acheter. Seulement puisqu'on parle d'un nouveau procédé pour fixer le pastel serait peutetre sage de lui demander de fixer de cette façon en cas d'achat. Poignée de main à toi et ta Koning

Vincent

7 Letter 477 from Vincent van Gogh to his brother Theo, April 1888,
with a sketch of his painting *Blossoming Pear Tree* (Plate 21), JH1395

from life itself, prevented his work from becoming sentimental: ' The peasant *must* be a peasant, that digger *must* dig' (Letter 418, July 1885). In pursuit of the 'startling realism' achieved by the contemporary illustrators that had absorbed his attention in London, he went on to expand this idea: 'To draw *a peasant's figure in action*, I repeat, that's what an essentially modern figure is, the very core of modern art, which neither the Greeks nor the Renaissance nor the old Dutch school have done.'

Unswerving in his belief that '*people* are more important than anything else' van Gogh's love of landscape at first took second place to the exacting programme he set himself of studying the figure in the hope of making a living by illustration. His only means of support came from his brother Theo, who, like him, had followed his uncles into art dealing. Yet despite Theo's generosity, Vincent could never organize his finances to pay for all the peasant models he required. When money ran out he turned to pure nature for refreshment, concentrating on the landscape settings for his workaday scenes, with reassuring results:
'More and more I feel that drawing the figure is a good thing which indirectly has a good influence on drawing landscape. If one draws a willow as if it were a living being – and after all, it really is – then the surroundings follow in due course if one has concentrated all one's attention only on that same tree, not giving up until one has put some life into it.'
(Letter 152, October 1881)

Van Gogh worked largely in isolation, and the personification of the natural world reflected in this passage suggests the close relationship in which he saw himself with nature. From time to time he identified it as some opponent to be tamed or from which to wrest a secret; or as a mistress, 'Dame Nature or Reality', to be courted:
'Nature always begins by resisting the artist, but he who really takes it seriously does not allow that resistance to put him off his stride; on the contrary, it is that much more of a stimulus to fight for victory, and at bottom nature and a true artist agree. Nature certainly is "intangible", yet one must seize her, and with a strong hand. And then after one has struggled and wrestled with nature, sometimes she becomes a little more docile and yielding.'
(Letter 152, October 1881)

8 *Vase with Daisies and Anemones*. 1887.
Oil, 61 × 38 cm (24 × 15 in).
State Museum Kröller-Müller, Otterlo, F323 JH1295

Van Gogh had shown little head for abstractions of an academic kind, but, immersed in the
practical business of drawing and painting, his conscientiousness paid off and he described to
Theo his attempt to make a lively rendering of a patch of woodland:
'It struck me how sturdily those little stems were rooted in the ground. I began painting them
with a brush, but because the surface was already so heavily covered, a brush stroke was lost in
it – then I squeezed the roots and trunks in from the tube, and modelled it a little with the
brush. Yes – now they stand there rising from the ground, strongly rooted in it.... I see that
nature has told me something, has spoken to me, and that I have put it down in shorthand...
and it is not the tame or conventional language derived from a studied manner or a system
rather than from nature itself.' (Letter 228, September 1882)

Apart from the private instruction he received briefly from Mauve in 1881–2 and some six weeks
spent at the Antwerp Academy in 1886, van Gogh was entirely self-taught, learning his trade
more effectively, he felt, by spontaneous and unconventional methods. If he could assert that 'it is
not the language of painters but the language of nature which one should listen to' (Letter 218,
July 1882), he was ready, nonetheless, to find support for his ideas in the work of other artists.

Admired practitioners with the brush were artists such as Rembrandt, Ruysdael and Frans
Hals, who 'dashed off a thing from the first stroke and did not retouch very much'. By such
means Hals and Rembrandt created 'hands that lived, but were not finished in the sense they
demand nowadays' (Letter 427, October 1885). Searching for ways of translating what he saw
and felt into paint, van Gogh wrote to Theo that he had come across a passage about
Gainsborough which again stimulated him to work with one stroke. He quoted the passage:
'It is this brusqueness of touch that produces so much effect. The spontaneity of his impression
is all there, and communicates itself to the spectator. For the rest Gainsborough had a perfect
method of ensuring the completeness of his composition. He planned his picture all at once,
and carried it out harmoniously from top to bottom, without concentrating his attention on
separate little fragments, without obstinately worrying over details, for he sought the general
effect, and he nearly always found it, thanks to his broad vision on the canvas, which he looked
at as one looks at nature, at a single glance.' (Letter 435, November 1885)

While he was in the Netherlands, van Gogh continually strove to create a three-dimensional palpitating reality, either with brush or pencil. From his scrutiny of painters like Hals, Rubens and others, he saw that colour as well as the vitality of the artist's drawing could be used to express form. But whereas drawing was in the control of artists and could, he felt, be safely left to the guidance of 'that conscience which is called sentiment, their soul', the visual properties of the pigments, were, like the workings of nature itself, something to be learnt. He immersed himself in a study of Delacroix's colour theories, and the buzz of excited thoughts that accompanied his new findings even led him, as he told Theo, to question the springs of creativity:

'The *laws* of the colours are unutterably beautiful, just because they are *not accidental*. In the same way that people nowadays no longer believe in fantastic *miracles*, no longer believe in a God who capriciously and despotically flies from one thing to another, but begin to feel more respect and admiration for and faith in nature – in the same way, and for the same reasons, I think that in art, the old-fashioned idea of innate genius, inspiration, etc., I do not say must be put aside, but thoroughly reconsidered, verified – and greatly modified. However, I do not deny the existence of genius, or even its being innate. But I certainly do deny the inference that theory and instruction should, as a matter of course, always be useless.'
(Letter 371, June 1884)

In fact, his aim in matters of both drawing and colour were identical: to avoid 'realism in the sense of *literal* truth, namely *exact* drawing and local colour' (Letter 402, April 1885). It was not that he saw nature in opposition to his ideas on painting, but that, in the final collaboration, it was up to the artist to orchestrate the masterpiece. 'My great longing is to learn to make those very incorrectnesses, those deviations, remodellings, changes in reality, so that they may become, yes, lies if you like – but truer than the literal truth' (Letter 418, July 1885). As he explained elsewhere: 'I study nature, so as not to do foolish things, to remain reasonable; however, I don't care so much whether my colour is exactly the same, as long as it looks beautiful on my canvas, as beautiful as it looks in nature.' (Letter 429, October 1885)

Van Gogh made a vain attempt to learn the piano in order to understand the connections

9 *Garden with Sunflowers*. 1888.
Pencil, reed pen and brown ink, 60 × 48.5 cm (23⅝ × 19¼ in).
National Museum Vincent van Gogh, Amsterdam, F1457 JH1539

Delacroix drew between the calculated effects of colour harmonies in music and in painting. He spoke rapturously of a splendid 'symphony' of colour, 'simple, and infinitely deep as nature is herself' and he clearly had abstract or symbolic colour values in mind when he considered ways of evoking the sensations aroused by each season:
'Spring is tender, green young corn and pink apple blossoms.
Autumn is the contrast of the yellow leaves with violet tones.
Winter is the snow with the black silhouettes.
But now, if summer is the contrast of blues with an element of orange in the golden bronze of the corn, one could paint a picture which expressed the mood of the seasons in each of the contrasts of the complementary colours (red and green, blue and orange, yellow and violet, white and black).' (Letter 372, July 1884)

The practical application of van Gogh's reflections on colour received its greatest stimulus when he moved to France in 1886, first to Paris and then to Arles. In Paris he came into contact for the first time with the Impressionists and their work, among them Renoir and Monet. His palette, which six months before had been 'thawing', now burst suddenly and brilliantly into bloom in a large number of colourful flower-pieces. It is from this year, 1886, until his death in 1890, a brief but amazingly rich five-year period, that all the paintings in this book are drawn.

In 1888, still in search of colour, van Gogh travelled south as far as Arles in Provence. But instead of the anticipated 'land of the *blue* tones and gay colours', he found sky and countryside white with snow 'like the winter landscapes of the Japanese'. His propensity to link landscape and art was now spurred by the images on Japanese woodblock prints, which he had begun to acquire in Antwerp. When he was given a free run of the store amassed in Paris by the businessman and Orientalist Siegfried Bing, van Gogh's collecting became a passion. Impressed by the calm and simple way of life described in the prints, he imagined that, once in Provence, he had come south to the equivalent of Japan, where people 'live in nature as though they themselves were flowers'. He expected that here his own life would 'become more and more like a Japanese painter's, living close to nature like a petty tradesman' (Letter 540, September 1888).

10 *Vase with Pink Roses*. 1890.
Oil, 93 × 72 cm (36⅝ × 28⅜ in).
From the private collection of Mr and Mrs Walter H. Annenberg, F682 JH1979

11

ORCHARD WITH BLOSSOMING PLUM TREES

1888. Reed pen heightened with white, 39.5 × 54 cm
(15³/₄ × 21¹/₄in)

National Museum Vincent van Gogh, Amsterdam, F1414 JH1385

'These drawings were made with a reed sharpened
the way you would a goose quill; I intend to make a
series of them, and hope to do better ones than the
first two. It is a method that I had already tried in
Holland some time ago, but I hadn't such good
reeds there as here.' (Letter 478, April 1888)
'Sometimes I regret that I cannot make up my mind
to work more at home and extemporary. The
imagination is certainly a faculty which we must
develop, one which alone can lead us to the creation
of a more exalting and consoling nature than the
single brief glance at reality – which in our sight is
ever changing, passing like a flash of lightning – can
let us perceive.... Working directly on the spot all the
time, I try to grasp what is essential in the drawing –
later I fill in the spaces which are bounded by
contours – either expressed or not, but in any case
felt – with tones which are also simplified.'
(Letter B3, to Émile Bernard, April 1888)

Working full tilt, out of doors whatever the weather, in direct confrontation with the motif, van Gogh sensed a change in himself, which he attributed to the influence of Oriental perceptions: 'One's sight changes: you see things with an eye more Japanese, you feel colour differently. The Japanese draw quickly, very quickly, like a lightning flash, because their nerves are finer, their feeling simpler.' (Letter 500, June 1888)

Van Gogh spent just over a year in Arles, leaving in May 1889 to enter an asylum in Saint-Rémy as a voluntary patient, following the psychological crisis in which he cut off part of his ear. The paintings he made during this period owe their emotional intensity to the fine-tuning of his rapid and, by now, very assured style. With it he gave us a unique interpretation of the character of the south of France: its clarity of light which opened up and drew into focus great dizzying distances and which described the flattened shapes of objects with shadowless brilliance; the relentless sunshine that emblazoned the town and landscape with gold and brought heightened colour juxtapositions into play on his canvas; the intense cobalt blue of the night sky that made the stars appear to him 'more sparklingly gemlike than at home – even in Paris: opals you might call them, emeralds, lapis lazuli, rubies, sapphires' (Letter 499, June 1888); the heat that made a garden of multi-coloured flowers shimmer and vibrate like a Monticelli bouquet (Pl. 35); the landscape itself which suggested one of his most optimistic and resonant images, that of the reaper in the field of wheat: 'it is an image of death as the great book of nature speaks of it,' van Gogh wrote. 'But there's nothing sad in this death, it goes its way in broad daylight with a sun flooding everything with a light of pure gold.'
(Letter 604, September 1889)

Referring to the progress he made with his work, van Gogh frequently used the analogy of a seed sown and brought diligently to mature growth. When his life was cut short tragically by his own hand at the age of thirty-seven, he had sold just one painting. To an artist so utterly convinced of what he was about that, as he said, 'I shall try to reach it even at the risk of my own life', his lack of commercial success was a continual disappointment, for which he felt the uncritical speculation of the art market was largely to blame:
'Those high prices one hears about, paid for work of painters who are dead and who were never

12 *Augustine Roulin (La Berceuse)*. 1889.
Oil, 92 × 73 cm (36¼ × 28¾ in).
State Museum Kröller-Müller, Otterlo, F504 JH1655

paid so much while they were alive, it is a kind of tulip trade, under which the living painters suffer rather than gain any benefit. And it will also disappear like the tulip trade.
But one may reason that, though the tulip trade has long been gone and is forgotten, the flower growers have remained and will remain. And thus I consider painting too, thinking that what abides is like a kind of flower growing. And as far as it concerns me, I reckon myself happy to be in it.' (Letter 612, to his mother, October 1889)

A year after van Gogh's death the critic Octave Mirbeau devoted a leading article to him in *L'Echo de Paris*, an avant-garde literary and political journal. It described an artist who might have won Zola's admiration because he painted according to his own eyes and his own disposition: 'Not always literally exact, or rather never exact, for one sees nature through one's own temperament,' as van Gogh himself put it (Letter 399, April 1885). Van Gogh had eyes for nature that lifted him, on occasion, into mystical transports of delight, but he believed that the artist had a duty, in any case, to be fully absorbed by nature in order to apprehend its truth. He read the great book of nature as he had once read the Book itself. And yet, Mirbeau wrote, in attempting to grasp the measure of his achievement, 'he was not absorbed by nature either. He had absorbed nature into himself; he had forced it to unbend, to mould itself into the shapes of his thoughts, to follow him in his flights, even to submit to his highly characteristic deformations.... He spares no effort, to the benefit of the trees, skies, flowers and fields, which he inflates with the astonishing dream of his being.'

THE PLATES

❁

13
PINK PEACH TREES

1888. Oil, 73 × 59.5 cm (28 3/4 × 23 5/8 in)

State Museum Kröller-Müller, Otterlo, F394 JH1379

Van Gogh arrived in the south of France in February 1888 to find the landscape he had envisaged as one of bright colour under a strong sun still wrapped in snow. Despite the bitter weather, he found Japanese motifs to paint in the winter scene and in knotty branches of almond just bursting into bud (*see* Pl. 1). By the end of March a gloriously fine spell brought the orchards of peach, plum, apple, pear and apricot into bloom together and van Gogh was bubbling with excitement: 'I'm up to my ears in work, for the trees are in blossom and I want to paint a Provençal orchard of astounding gaiety,' he wrote to Theo (Letter 473). And he dashed off an impassioned letter to his friend, the painter Émile Bernard, as well:

'At the moment I am absorbed in the blooming fruit trees, pink peach trees, yellow-white pear trees. My brush stroke has no system at all. I hit the canvas with irregular touches of the brush, which I leave as they are. Patches of thickly laid-on colour, spots of canvas left uncovered, here and there portions that are left absolutely unfinished, repetitions, savageries; in short, I am inclined to think that the result is so disquieting and irritating as to be a godsend to those people who have fixed preconceived ideas about technique.... In short, my dear comrade, in no case an eye-deceiving job.'
(Letter B3)

The painting of these peach trees is certainly not concerned with 'eye-deceiving', or photographic realism. Van Gogh has captured his own exhilaration and the freshness and beauty of spring in a 'frenzy of impastos', the branches sprouting tongues in every shade of pink from deep crimson to palest rose 'against a sky of glorious blue and white'. He pronounced it 'probably the best landscape I have done'. When on 30 March he was sent an obituary of his mentor Anton Mauve (1838-88), which he thought failed to do Mauve justice, he was moved to pay personal tribute: 'Something – I don't know what – took hold of me and brought a lump to my throat, and I wrote on my picture: SOUVENIR DE MAUVE – VINCENT THEO' (Letter 472, March 1888).

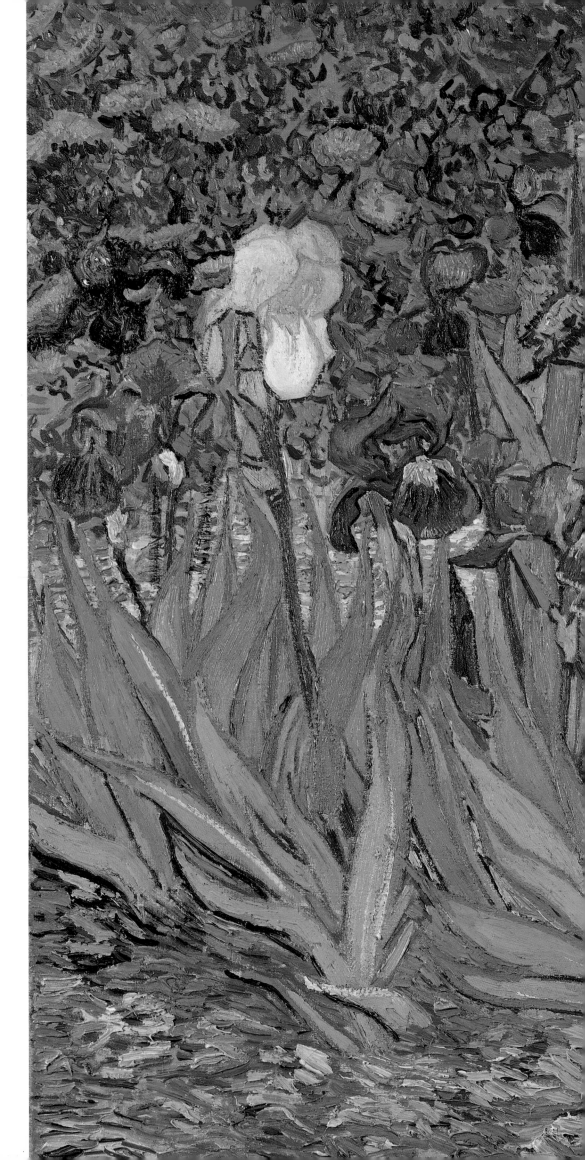

14
IRISES

1889. Oil, 71 × 93 cm (28 × 36 ⅝ in)
Private collection, F608 JH1691

'Romance and romanticism are of our time, and painters must have imagination and sentiment. Fortunately realism and naturalism are not free from it. Zola creates, but does not hold up a *mirror* to things, he creates *wonderfully*, but *creates*, *poetizes*, that is why it is so beautiful.... One starts with a hopeless struggle to follow nature, and everything goes wrong; one ends by calmly creating from one's palette, and nature agrees with it, and follows. But these two opposites cannot be separated. The drudging, though it may seem futile, gives an intimacy with nature, a sounder knowledge of things. And a beautiful saying of Doré's (who sometimes is so clever!) is, *Je me souviens*. Though I believe that the best pictures are more or less freely painted by heart, I *can't* help adding that one can never study nature too much and too hard. The greatest, most powerful imaginations have at the same time made things directly from nature that strike one dumb.' (Letter 429, October 1885)

15

BLOSSOMING BRANCHES

1890. Pencil, reed pen, brown ink, 41 × 31 cm (16¹/₈ × 12¹/₄ in)

National Museum Vincent van Gogh, Amsterdam,
F1612 JH2059

16

DEATH'S-HEAD MOTH ON AN ARUM

1889. Oil, 33 × 24 cm (13 × 9¹/₂ in)

National Museum Vincent van Gogh, Amsterdam,
F610 JH1702

Van Gogh's closely observed drawings of insects reflect his devotion to wild life, as well as his familiarity with the teeming pages in Yoshimaro's *A New Book of Insects*. In his painting these creatures enhanced his imaginative colour compositions, like the swarm of 'big blue flies, emerald rose beetles and cicadas' (Letter 614a) encircling the olive orchards, which he saw as a haze of blue continuous with the flowering trees and sky. Butterflies likewise contributed picturesque flashes of contrasting colour and his depiction of what was probably an Emperor, not a Death's-Head Hawk Moth, is unusually graphic in its detail. Catching sight of it in the asylum garden at Saint-Rémy, van Gogh was clearly bewitched by its lavish markings, which he matched with vigorous drawing in the arum plants: 'Yesterday I drew a very big, rather rare night moth, called the death's head, its colouring of amazing distinction, black, grey, cloudy white tinged with carmine or vaguely shading off into olive-green; it is very big. I had to kill it to paint it, and it was a pity, the beastie was so beautiful. I will send you the drawing along with some other drawings of plants.'
(Letter 592, 25 May 1889)
One of these drawings, probably of the same arum patch (*see* endpapers), was done with a reed pen, which van Gogh now handled deftly and inventively. *Blossoming Branches* is typical of his unpretentious rendering of plants and wild flowers placed simply on a white page. It was one of the independent drawings done in the north of France, in Auvers, in the last months of his life, June/July 1890.

17

VASE WITH VIOLET IRISES AGAINST A
YELLOW BACKGROUND (detail)

1890. Oil, 92 × 73.5 cm (36¼ × 29⅛ in)

National Museum Vincent van Gogh, Amsterdam,
F678 JH1977

During his time in the asylum of Saint-Paul-de-
Mausole in Saint-Rémy van Gogh suffered several
relapses which confined him to the grounds of the
institution, and in a letter to Theo he gave vent to his
feelings of frustration:
'My surroundings here begin to weigh on me more
than I can say – my word, I have been patient for
more than a year – I need air, I feel overwhelmed
with boredom and grief.... I assure you it is
something to resign yourself to living under
surveillance, even supposing it were sympathetic,
and to sacrifice your liberty, keep yourself out of
society, and have nothing but your work without any
distraction.' (Letter 631, May 1890)
Nevertheless, work in itself provided a soothing
distraction. With his mind set on going north to
refresh his flagging spirits, his renewed optimism
and energy burst out in a group of resplendent
flower-pieces, two of roses and two of irises:
'At present all goes well, the whole horrible attack
has disappeared like a thunderstorm and I am
working to give a last stroke of the brush here with a
calm and steady enthusiasm. I am doing a canvas of
roses with a light green background and two
canvases representing big bunches of violet irises,
one lot against a pink background in which the effect
is soft and harmonious because of the combination of
greens, pinks, violets [Pl. 31]. On the other hand,
the other violet bunch (ranging from carmine to
pure Prussian blue) stands out against a startling
citron background, with other yellow tones in the
vase and the stand on which it rests, so it is an effect
of tremendously disparate complementaries, which
strengthen each other by their juxtaposition.' (Letter
633, May 1890)
Violet and yellow offered a radiant and emotive
colour contrast that van Gogh had already relished
in two earlier paintings, in *The Sower* and in a
prospect of Arles from the south with a ditch of irises
in the foreground – 'a little town surrounded by
fields all covered with yellow and purple flowers;
exactly – can't you see it? – like a Japanese dream'
(Letter 487, May 1888).

18

FIELD OF GRASS WITH DANDELIONS AND TREE TRUNKS

1890. Oil, 72 × 90 cm (28³/₈ × 35³/₈ in)

State Museum Kröller-Müller, Otterlo, F676 JH1970

Van Gogh's most prolonged bout of illness in
Saint-Rémy struck in February during
blossom-time, just after he had finished a
large outdoor painting of almond branches to
celebrate the birth of his nephew Vincent (Pl.
2). 'My work was going well,' he wrote to
Theo two months later, 'the last canvas of
branches in blossom – you will see that it was
perhaps the best, the most patiently worked
thing I had done, painted with calm and with
a greater firmness of touch. And the next day,
down like a brute.' (Letter 628, April 1890)
No wonder van Gogh felt out of luck, for on
his recovery the blossom had dropped.
    Instead he set to work on the spring
landscape of the asylum grounds, telling
Theo that 'as soon as I got out into the park,
I got back all my lucidity for work; I have
more ideas in my head than I could ever
carry out, but without it clouding my mind.
The brush strokes come like clockwork.'
(Letter 630, May 1890)
He sketched the view illustrated here, in a
letter to Theo: 'I have done two canvases of
the fresh grass in the park, one of which is
extremely simple, here is a hasty sketch of it.
The trunk of a pine violet-pink and then the
grass with white flowers and dandelions, a
little rose tree and other tree trunks in the
background right at the top of the canvas.'
(Letter 631, May 1890)
In this beautiful and straightforward
treatment of undergrowth flooded with
sunlight, the variant rhythms of the
landscape seem to come instinctively to van
Gogh's brush. The pervasive tranquillity of
the scene epitomizes what he experienced as
'the purer nature of a countryside compared
with the suburbs and cabarets of Paris'
(Letter 595, June 1889).

VASE WITH PEONIES AND ROSES (detail)

1886. Oil, 59 × 71 cm (23$\frac{1}{4}$ × 28 in)

State Museum Kröller Müller, Otterlo, F249 JH1105

Whether he was looking deep into the heart of a flower through its compact formation of petals, into a dense entanglement of stems and leaves, at a web of branches silhouetted against the sky, or at the idiosyncratic stance of a tree, we encounter van Gogh listening, intently as always, to the language of nature as he had first heard it in the Netherlands.

There he had taught himself to translate it rigorously and with painstaking effort into drawing, and then to brush life into it with paint. When he recognized something in his interpretation that spoke 'straight from my own heart', he sensed that he had taken an encouraging step forwards.

By the time he reached Paris in 1886, his delight in Delacroix's theories and in Rubens' handling of colour had sharpened his own chromatic sensibility, and he concentrated on expressing his immediate feeling for nature in terms of colour as well as line. Characteristically he saw progress towards his new goal from both a commercial and an artistic viewpoint, and he wrote hopefully of his chances to his English painter friend Horace Mann Livens: 'With much energy, with a sincere personal feeling of colour in nature I would say an artist can get on here notwithstanding the many obstructions' (Letter 459a, August-October 1886).

Flowers provided him with an obvious source of colour for his experiments, of which *Vase with Peonies and Roses* is characteristic of some of his early harmonies. Richly composed in deep reds and greens, it still relies on a dark ground to set off a froth of pink, white and cream petals. Both tone and compositional arrangement recall the work of Courbet and of Fantin-Latour, whose *Still Life with Flowers* of 1877 formed part of the collection made by the two van Gogh brothers, Vincent and Theo.

20
JUG WITH RED AND WHITE CARNATIONS

1886. Oil, 40 × 52 cm (15³/₄ × 20¹/₂ in)

State Museum Kröller-Müller, Otterlo, F327 JH1126

Van Gogh stayed in Paris with his brother Theo, who by July 1886 was able to write reassuringly to their mother:
'You wouldn't recognize Vincent, so much he has changed and it strikes others even more than me. He has had a major operation to his mouth, for he had nearly lost all his teeth as a result of the bad state of his stomach. The doctor says that he has now completely got over it. He is progressing tremendously in his work and this is proved by the fact that he is becoming successful. He has not yet sold paintings for money, but is exchanging his work for other pictures. In that way we obtain a fine collection which, of course, also has a certain value. There is a dealer in pictures who has now taken four of his paintings and has promised him to arrange for an exhibition of his work next year. He is mainly painting flowers – with the object to put a more lively colour into his next pictures. He is also much more cheerful than in the past and people like him here. To give you proof: hardly a day passes or he is asked to come to the studios of well-known painters, or they come to see him. He also has acquaintances who give him a collection of flowers every week which may serve him as models. If they are able to keep it up I think his difficult times are over and he will be able to make it by himself.'
This gracefully balanced spray of flowers, which may well have been among those given van Gogh by friends, allowed him to exploit his favourite opposition of red and green, but now in a much lighter, brighter key.

BLOSSOMING PEAR TREE

1888. Oil, 73 × 46 cm (28³/₄ × 18¹/₈ in)

State Museum Vincent van Gogh, Amsterdam,
F405 JH1394

'Every day is a good day now,' van Gogh wrote to his brother from Arles, and enclosed one of his many urgent requests for more paints so that he could catch the fruit trees in blossom. The ever-supportive Theo dispatched the order promptly, to van Gogh's evident delight:

'I am so glad to have them.... This morning I worked on an orchard of plum trees in bloom; all at once a fierce wind sprang up, an effect I had never seen before, and returned at intervals. The sun shone in between, and all the little white flowers sparkled. It was so lovely. My friend the Dane came to join me, and I went on painting at the risk and peril of seeing the whole show on the ground at any moment – it's a white effect with a good deal of yellow in it, and blue and lilac, the sky white and blue. But as to the execution of what one paints outside like this, what will people say?' (Letter 476, April 1888)

The jubilant van Gogh worked on compulsively despite the irritation of the mistral, and no doubt wiping quite a few petals off palette and canvas in the process. But there is evidence, too, of carefully considered plans for pictures conceived in series of threes, as part of a much larger decorative scheme of orchards he would continue the following season. *Blossoming Pear Tree* was to be the centre-piece of one of these groups and consequently it received more deliberate finish: 'I have also just now a little pear tree, vertical, between two horizontal canvases. That will make six canvases of orchards in bloom. I am now trying every day to touch them up and give them a certain unity' (Letter 477, April 1888). He sketched the tree with detailed colour notes in the same letter (Pl. 7):

'The ground violet, in the background a wall with straight poplars and a very blue sky. The little pear tree has a violet trunk and white flowers, with a big yellow butterfly on one of the clusters. To the left in the corner, a little garden with a fence of yellow reeds, and green bushes, and a flower bed. A little pink house.'

22

IRISES

1889. Oil on paper mounted on canvas,
62.5 × 48 cm (24³/₄ × 18⁷/₈ in)

National Gallery of Canada, Ottawa, F601 JH1699

'Since I have been here, the deserted garden, planted with large pines beneath which the grass grows tall and unkempt and mixed with various weeds, has sufficed for my work, and I have not yet gone outside,' van Gogh wrote to Theo in late May 1889, soon after his arrival at Saint-Rémy (Letter 592). And he added that 'considering my life is spent mostly in the garden, it is not so unhappy'. Among the many beautiful and arresting subjects he discovered were irises, roses, lilac and one of those hidden corners in the garden 'which represents the eternal nests of greenery for lovers. Some thick tree trunks covered with ivy, the ground also covered with ivy and periwinkle, a stone bench and a bush of pale roses in the cold shadow. In the foreground some plants with white calyxes. It is green, violet and pink.'

Once again flowers provided the material for colour effects, with which van Gogh conjured poetry from the most unassuming of themes, such as this iris plant growing among tufts of rough grass. His concern was to bring 'style' to a portrayal of the simple, humble and everyday and, on this occasion, a patch of untended ground becomes an arena for a vigorous pattern of brushstrokes and harmoniously placed colour contrasts. Yet, the effect remains triumphantly that of the outdoors and is in no way self-conscious. The painting pursued a theme he had already treated once before in Arles and, even more lavishly, in his painting of a large, sprawling clump of violet irises (Pl. 14).

In this last, the areas of colour, with a single white 'rest', are more distinctly divided into violet irises, marigolds, red earth and green 'sword-like leaves', on which, as the critic Félix Fénéon commented, 'the "Irises"violently slash their petals to pieces'. It is more likely that van Gogh was attracted to the flower because of its serenely naturalistic depiction in Japanese popular prints, rather than because it suggested any such dramatic imagery.

23
PINK ROSES

1890. Oil, 32 × 40.5 cm (12⁵/₈ × 16¹/₈ in)

Ny Carlsberg Glyptotek, Copenhagen, F595 JH2009

'You will remember that we saw a magnificent garden of roses by Renoir. I was expecting to find subjects like that here.... You would probably have to go to Nice to find Renoir's gardens again. I have seen very few roses here, though there are some, among them the big red roses called Rose de Provence.' (Letter 488, May 1888)

The scarcity of roses van Gogh commented on when he came south to Arles accounts for their surprising absence in his early Provençal canvases. Roses were familiar subject-matter in his contemporaries' work, whereas the irises van Gogh painted were an uncommon choice among European artists. No doubt his enthusiasm for the woodblock prints of Japanese artists such as Hokusai provided the initial inspiration for depicting the iris, although as he told his younger sister, Wil: 'I don't need Japanese pictures here, for I am always telling myself *that here I am in Japan*. Which means that I have only to open my eyes and paint what is right in front of me, if I think it effective' (Letter W7, September 1888). Irises abounded, growing wild in the ditches round Arles.

Van Gogh discovered the theme of roses in the garden of the asylum of Saint-Rémy. The two still lifes he painted while he was a patient there were intended as pendants to vases of irises (Pls. 17, 31). He returned to the theme the following month in Auvers-sur-Oise, just north of Paris, where the lush abundance of wild and garden flowers and the softer northern light inspired the massed arrangement of pink roses illustrated opposite. The green bowl is barely indicated and the roses spill over their container's edge in blowsy profusion. Van Gogh's angled viewpoint suggests that he may have been visualizing the roses as he had seen them growing, possibly in the garden of his physician Dr Gachet, and their natural sprawl makes a telling contrast with the grandly composed still-life portraits (*see* Pl. 10).

24

BRANCHES OF FLOWERING ACACIA

1890. Oil, 33 × 24 cm (13 × 9^1/$_2$ in)

Nationalmuseum, Stockholm, F821 JH2015

These branches of flowering acacia, or mimosa, with their yellow flowers and silvery leaves were painted in Auvers. Swiftly executed on coarse canvas in a bold diagonal composition, van Gogh uses a welter of impressionist marks to create the character of mimosa, its flowers falling loosely and untidily in long panicles. The broad impasto brushstrokes are almost abstract in effect, combining yellows, lilacs and white against blue-black, with hints of green and touches of pink. In mood it is very reminiscent of the dramatic night skies van Gogh painted in the south of France, in which coloured stars seemed to him to radiate hope from a dark infinity.

The unnaturalistic colour suggests that this picture may even have been painted by evening light, a time which particularly appealed to van Gogh for its intimate atmosphere. On the other hand, the subdued colours may express his wish to return to the muted half-tones and dark/light contrasts of his earlier period in Nuenen, Holland. At that time he was painting a number of still lifes of birds' nests on plain grounds and he explained to Theo that they were 'purposely painted against a black background, because I want it to be obvious in these studies that the objects do not appear in their natural surroundings, but against a conventional background. A *living* nest in nature is quite different – one hardly sees the nest itself, one sees the birds.' (Letter 428, October 1885)

If the branches of flowering acacia were cut rather than painted as they grew, did van Gogh intend to make a similar distinction? Or was he striving for the shimmering effect of silver and gold that had once caught his imagination in the olive orchards in Arles?

JAPANESE VASE WITH ROSES AND ANEMONES

1890. Oil, 51 x 51 cm (20^1/$_8$ × 20^1/$_8$ in)

Musée d'Orsay, Paris, F764 JH2045

During the last months of his life in Auvers, van Gogh relied heavily on the friendship and sympathy of the doctor supervising his health, Paul-Ferdinand Gachet, and he confided to Theo: 'Now nothing, absolutely nothing, is keeping us here but Gachet – but he will remain a friend, I should think. I feel that I can do not too bad a picture every time I go to his house, and he will continue to ask me to dinner every Sunday or Monday' (Letter 638, June 1890). Although van Gogh complained about the size of the meals, he clearly derived pleasure from the company of this informed, if eccentric art lover, owner of 'a *very* fine Pissarro' and 'two fine flower pieces by Cézanne'. He reported that Gachet's house was 'full of black antiques, black, black, black, except for the impressionist pictures mentioned' (Letter 635, May 1890). The atmosphere clearly weighed on him for he repeated that it was 'full, full like an antique dealer's, of things that are not always interesting. But nevertheless there is this advantage, there is always something for arranging flowers in or for a still life'. (Letter 638)

In return for the doctor's kindness, van Gogh painted his portrait and that of his daughter, as well as his house and garden, and he also made a number of paintings of flowers, including several still lifes in vases. One of the admired Cézannes may have suggested the rounded table edges, complementing bulbous vases and simplified, schematic flower forms, to be seen in several flower-pieces at this time.

By contrast, the bright colours in the painting illustrated here evoke the light-hearted Oriental mood he was always in quest of and symbolized here by the knotted branch on the Japanese vase. The composition, with its assertively angled table top and curiously jutting rose stem, clearly takes its cue from the shape of the vase, while the painting of the flowers invokes the decorative stylized shapes pictured in Japanese prints.

26

FIELDS WITH POPPIES

1889. Oil, 71 × 91 cm (28 × 35⅞ in)

Kunsthalle, Bremen, F581 JH1751

It may seem surprising that a man who came from a land famous for its colourful fields of tulips painted them only once, but it should be remembered that van Gogh's excitement with colour was only just emerging as he left for Paris in 1886. When Claude Monet painted the tulip fields on a visit to Holland in the same year, he regretted the fact that the artist's palette was so inadequate in rendering the brilliance of natural hues and it is interesting to speculate on what van Gogh, with his more systematic colour theories, would have made of the same glorious patchwork, had he returned to the Netherlands. Both artists, however, delighted in capturing the dazzling effects of wild poppies and van Gogh may have been aware of Monet's atmospheric painting of poppies near Giverny before he went south.

His rapturous response to the 'exquisite' colour and 'rich green' foliage of Provence, 'the like of which we seldom see in the North', was tempered by his surprise at 'the scarcity of flowers; there are no cornflowers in the wheat, and seldom poppies' (Letter 502, June 1888). To his intense pleasure, he encountered flowers galore in the gardens and lush vegetation of Saint-Rémy, where he painted *Fields with Poppies*. Van Gogh had always had an eye for the picturesque attributes of countryside and he co-ordinated their visual variety in a rich and texturally animated tapestry of brushmarks.

TWELVE SUNFLOWERS IN A VASE

1888. Oil, 91 × 71 cm (35⁷/₈ × 28 in)
Neue Pinakothek, Munich, F456 JH1561

'You know that the peony is Jeannin's, the hollyhock belongs to Quost, but the sunflower is mine in a way,' van Gogh told Theo (Letter 573, January 1889), and for many people his name is associated uniquely with this flower.

His first drawings and paintings of sunflowers were made in 1887 in Paris where he saw them growing naturally in the cottage gardens around Montmartre. At the end of the season, as their heads faded and petals crumpled into flames around the ripening seed discs, he discovered one of his most fanciful still-life themes and one that evidently excited Gauguin's admiration. Starting from a simple harmony based on blue and yellow in *Two Cut Sunflowers, One Upside Down* (Pl. 28), he explored next the effect of a red ground and, in the last of a trio, *Four Cut Sunflowers, One Upside Down* (Pl. 4), he expanded the composition, enriching the orchestration of his palette with a flurry of flickering brushwork.

In Arles he returned to a more familiar interpretation, drawing a large bed of sunflowers 'in a little garden of a bathing establishment' (Pl. 9). Gradually the idea of the flower with its symbolic name and colour took hold of his imagination and came to represent all his hopes for a meaningful new life in the south, together with Gauguin and a flourishing studio of artists. In August 1888 he wrote to his friend Émile Bernard:

'I am thinking of decorating my studio with half a dozen pictures of "Sunflowers", a decoration in which the raw or broken chrome yellows will blaze forth on various backgrounds – blue, from the palest malachite green to *royal blue*, framed in thin strips of wood painted with orange lead.

Effects like those of stained-glass windows in a Gothic church.' (Letter B15)

A few days later a letter to Theo related:
'I am hard at it, painting with the enthusiasm of a Marseillais eating bouillabaisse.... I have three canvases going – 1st, three huge flowers in a green vase, with a light background, a size 15 canvas; 2nd, three flowers, one gone to seed, having lost its petals, and one a bud against a royal-blue background, size 25 canvas; 3rd, twelve flowers and buds in a yellow vase (size 30 canvas) [Pl. 27]. The last one is therefore light on light, and I hope it will be the best. Probably I shall not stop at that.' (Letter 526)

Indeed van Gogh was so pleased with these flower-pieces that he charged himself up to repeat the achievement the following year by making copies of them: 'Now to get up heat enough to melt that gold, those flower tones, it isn't everybody who can do it, it needs the whole and entire force and concentration of a single individual.' (Letter 573, January 1889)

Vase with Fourteen Sunflowers (Pl. 29) was one of these so-called replicas, but it was not identical to its original, now in the National Gallery in London (Pl. 6). The detail illustrated focuses on the manner in which van Gogh enlivened the flower centres with blue and red accents.

His extraordinary sense of colour correspondencies was central to his vision of natural harmony and it gave him the striking idea of hanging these glowing sunflowers, like 'candelabra' or the outer wings of a triptych, on either side of his portraits of *Augustine Roulin (La Berceuse)* (Pl. 12). 'And then the yellow and orange tones of the head will gain in brilliance by the proximity of the yellow wings.' (Letter 592, May 1889)

28

TWO CUT SUNFLOWERS, ONE UPSIDE DOWN

1887. Oil, 43 × 61 cm (16⁷/₈ × 24 in)

Metropolitan Museum of Art, New York, F375 JH1329

29

VASE WITH FOURTEEN SUNFLOWERS (detail)

1889. Oil, 95 × 73 cm (37³/₈ × 28³/₄ in)

National Museum Vincent van Gogh, Amsterdam,
F458 JH1667

30

VASE WITH POPPIES

1886. Oil, 56 × 46.5 cm (22 × 18¹/₂ in)

Wadsworth Atheneum, Hartford, Connecticut,
F279 JH1104

Van Gogh arrived in Paris towards the end of
February 1886. Living there was more costly than in
Antwerp and he was hard up. Nevertheless, that
summer he wrote in English to his friend H.M.
Livens that there were, in theory at least, more
opportunities to sell paintings in Paris and to
exchange pictures with fellow artists: 'With much
energy, with a sincere personal feeling of colour in
nature I would say an artist can get on here
notwithstanding the many obstructions. And I
intend remaining here still longer.' And he went on
to describe what he had been doing:
'I have lacked money for paying models else I had
entirely given myself to figure painting. But I have
made a series of color studies in painting, simply
flowers, red poppies, blue corn flowers and myosotys
[sic], white and rose roses, yellow
chrysanthemums – seeking oppositions of blue with
orange, red and green, yellow and violet seeking *les
tons rompus et neutres* to harmonise brutal extremes.
Trying to render intense colour and not a grey
harmony.
Now after these gymnastics I lately did two heads
which I dare say are better in light and colour than
those I did before.
So as we said at the time: in *colour* seeking *life* the
true drawing is modelling with colour.
I did a dozen landscapes too, frankly *green*
frankly *blue*.
And so I am struggling for life and progress in art.'
(Letter 459a, August to October 1887)
Van Gogh painted his first and most extensive group
of flower paintings during his stay in Paris in 1886
and 1887. The flower-piece illustrated and *Vase with
Poppies, Daisies, Cornflowers and Peonies* (Pl. 36), in
which red poppies are also the dominant element,
must have been two of his earliest colour exercises.

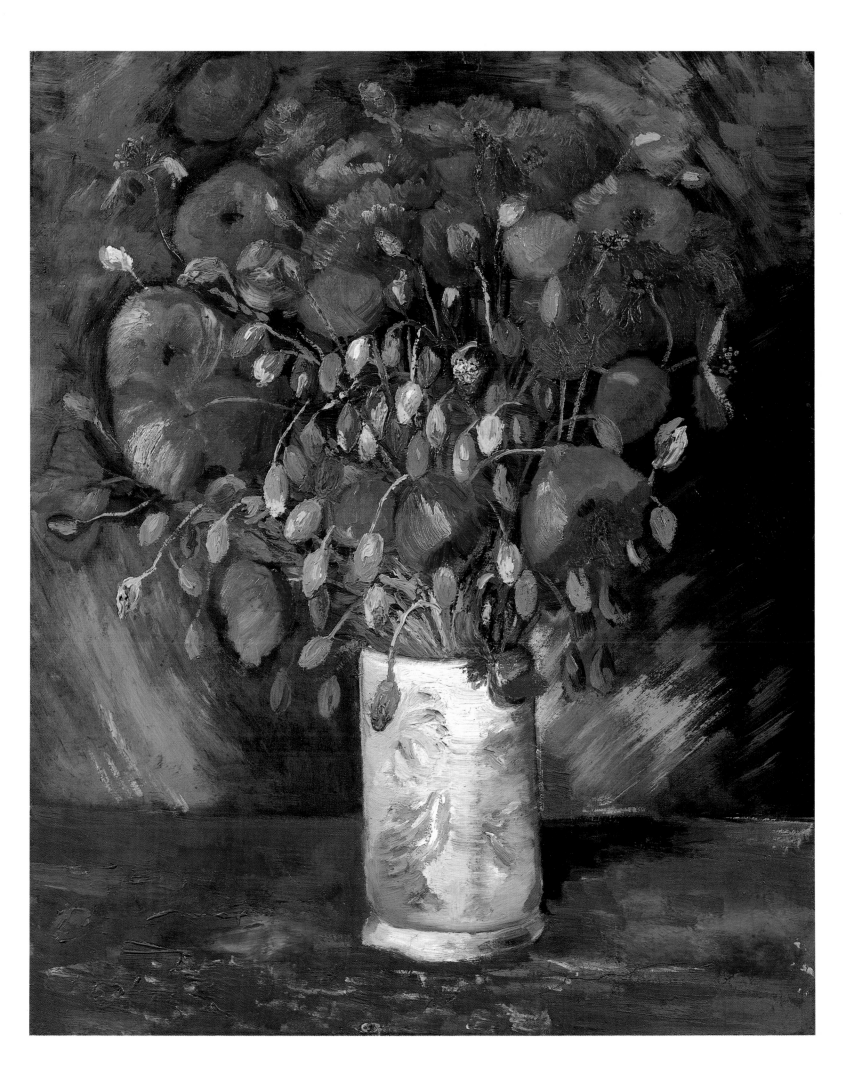

31

VASE WITH VIOLET IRISES AGAINST A PINK BACKGROUND

1890. Oil, 73 × 93 cm (28³/₄ × 36⁵/₈ in)

Metropolitan Museum of Art, New York, F680 JH1978

During the final days of his stay in the asylum of Saint-Rémy van Gogh was working 'like a man in a frenzy' on bunches of flowers. He wrote to the critic J.J. Isaäcson that 'these flowers are an avalanche of roses against a green background, and a very big bouquet of irises, violet against a yellow background, against a pink background' (Letter 614a, May 1890). Unfortunately the pink in the background of the bunch illustrated has sunk, thus depriving the painting of some of the warmth and gaiety of van Gogh's original conception, but its natural eloquence remains undiminished.

Van Gogh explained his creative deliberation as the act of listening to nature speak and a simultaneous, unrelenting effort to grasp its essential message with pencil or brush. 'It is the painter's duty to be entirely absorbed by nature and to use all his intelligence to express sentiment in his work so that it becomes intelligible to other people,' he wrote to Theo during his early struggles as an artist (Letter 221, July 1882). In the process he became one of nature's most ardent disciples and most passionate preachers. He interpreted it in a clear, down-to-earth manner, emulating those he felt to be completely in tune with nature – Zola, Cézanne, Millet and, of course, the Japanese. 'Millet is the voice of the wheat, and Jules Breton too,' he wrote in the same letter to Isaäcson.

For his part, van Gogh gave powerful and unparalleled expression to the sunflower and, from the equally joyful attention he paid to the iris, its colour complementing that of the sunflower, it can be said that his was the first Western voice to sing of the iris.

32

WILD ROSES WITH A BEETLE

1890. Oil, 32.5 × 23.5 cm (13 × 9¹/₂ in)

National Museum Vincent van Gogh, Amsterdam,
F749 JH2012

'Auvers is very beautiful, among other things a lot of old thatched roofs, which are getting rare...really it is profoundly beautiful, it is the real country, characteristic and picturesque, ' van Gogh wrote to Theo and his wife Jo on arrival in Auvers (Letter 635, May 1890). He was thankful to have left the city. 'Here one is far enough from Paris for it to be the real country, but nevertheless how changed it is since Daubigny. But not changed in an unpleasant way, there are many cottages and various modern middle-class dwellings very radiant and sunny and covered with flowers.'(Letter 637, May 1890)

As he settled down to work and recovered his serenity in the countryside he felt that it had done him good to go south, 'the better to see the North'. One of the sights he enjoyed in the North was the extravagant growth of roses with which he promptly filled several canvases. In the painting illustrated, he celebrates light, fresh air, luxuriant wildness and what the French writer Pierre Loti described as 'some free-and-easy beetle'. Loti's Japanese fantasy, *Madame Chrysanthème*, seems to have fascinated van Gogh and infused his romantic notion of life lived close to nature. Intrigued by small details of wildlife, he deeply respected the seriousness of artists like Karl Bodmer who devoted their lives to discovering the poetry hidden in nature's meanest manifestation.

'I admire and love the man who knew the whole forest of Fontainebleau, from the insect to the wild boar and from the stag to the lark, from the great oak and the rock mass to the fern and the blade of grass. Now a thing like that is not felt, nor even found by any chance comer.' (Letter 602, August 1889)

33

BRANCHES WITH WILD ROSES
(detail, enlarged)

1890. Oil, 23.5 × 32 cm (9^1/$_2$ × 12^5/$_8$ in)

National Museum Vincent van Gogh, Amsterdam,
F597 JH2011

'But just go and paint out-of-doors on the
spot itself! then all kinds of things happen; for
instance, I had to wipe off at least a hundred
or more flies from the four paintings you will
receive, not counting the dust and sand, not
counting that when one carries them across
the heath and through the hedges for several
hours, some thorns will scratch them, etc.
Not counting that when one arrives on the
heath after some hours' walk in this weather,
one is tired and exhausted from the heat.... I
don't know how it is with you, but as for
myself, the more I work in it, the more I get
absorbed in rural life.' (Letter 418, July 1885)

34

VASE WITH GLADIOLI

1886. Oil on canvas, 48.5 × 40 cm (19¹/₄ × 15³/₄ in)

National Museum Vincent van Gogh, F248a JH1148

While living in Nuenen in the south of Holland, from the end of 1883 to 1885, van Gogh had already studied the example of those 'colourists among colourists' – Frans Hals, Veronese, Rubens and Velázquez. Eugène Delacroix drew his special admiration and his theories on colour contrasts were of paramount importance to van Gogh's development: 'He makes us feel the life of things, and the expression, and the movement, that he *absolutely dominates his colours*' (Letter 439, December 1885). From now on colour was to dominate van Gogh's own thinking and the emotional impact of his painting: 'What colour is in a picture, enthusiasm is in life,' he wrote to Theo (Letter 443, January 1886).

Before he arrived in Paris van Gogh was only dimly aware of the colour experiments going on there: '*There is a school – I believe – of impressionists. But I know very little about it*' (Letter 402, April 1885). Once in the capital he quickly became familiar with the work of Monet, Sisley, Renoir and Degas, who showed their paintings on the Grand Boulevard, and, sympathizing with their natural and unconventional vision, he began seriously to apply his own colour theories using flowers as models. Gladioli featured in several arrangements in which he explored harmonies based on red, blue and yellow. The flowers in *Vase with Gladioli* were modelled entirely in colour using bold impasto strokes and dabs suggestive of gladioli florets. As shapes to paint, he clearly found the gladioli spikes rather stiff, for he usually disturbed their formality with wiry-stalked asters or bent stems, dangling over the side of the vase and lying on the table.

35

GARDEN WITH FLOWERS

1888. Oil, 72 × 91 cm (28³/₈ × 35⁷/₈ in)

Gemeentemuseum, The Hague (on loan from the
Netherlands Office for Fine Art), F429 JH1513

'Under the blue sky the orange, yellow, red
splashes of the flowers take on an amazing
brilliance, and in the limpid air there is a
something or other happier, more lovely than
in the North. It vibrates like the bouquet by
Monticelli which you have. I reproach myself
for not painting flowers here.... Oh, these
farm gardens, with their lovely big red
Provençal roses, and the vines and the fig
trees! It is all a poem, and the eternal bright
sunshine too, in spite of which the foliage
remains very green.' (Letter 519,
August 1888)

Van Gogh's joy in the sensations of summer
in Provence inspired several painted studies
and drawings of gardens, including that of a
bathing establishment (Pl. 9). In a letter to
his younger sister Wil the previous month he
described the scintillating effect of the garden
illustrated here:

'I have a study of a garden one metre wide,
poppies and other red flowers surrounded by
green in the foreground, and a square of blue
blowballs. Then a bed of orange and yellow
Africans, then white and yellow flowers, and
at last, in the background, pink and lilac, and
also dark violet scabiosas, and red
geraniums, and sunflowers, and a fig tree and
an oleander and a vine. And in the far
distance black cypresses against low white
houses with orange roofs – and a delicate
green-blue streak of sky.

Oh, I know very well that not a single flower
is drawn completely, that they are mere dabs
of colour, red, yellow, orange, green, blue,
violet, but the impression of all these colours
in their juxtaposition is there all right, in the
painting as in nature. But I suppose you
would be disappointed, and think it
unbeautiful, if you saw it. But you see that
the subject is rather summery.' (Letter W5)

36

VASE WITH POPPIES, DAISIES, CORNFLOWERS AND PEONIES

1886. Oil, 99 × 79 cm (39 × 31^1/$_8$ in)

State Museum Kröller-Müller, Otterlo, F278 JH1103

The exuberant colour in this profusion of field and garden flowers, stuffed into the vase and tumbling over the table, marks a complete change from the dark canvases van Gogh was painting in Antwerp and even from the low-keyed *Vase with Hollyhocks* (Pl. 3) painted in the same year. He was still experimenting with his palette, avoiding a slavish imitation of local colour and instead enjoying the freedom of colours 'which form a whole and harmonize, which stand out the more in contrast to another colour scheme' (Letter 429, October 1885). Van Gogh was clearly after effect.

The influence of the French Impressionists was beginning to make itself felt, although van Gogh admitted to H.M. Livens that 'since I saw the impressionists I assure you that neither your colour nor mine as it is developing [sic] itself, is *exactly* the same as their theories' (Letter 459a, August-October 1887). Apart from complementary oppositions, van Gogh still seems to be interested in the dark/light effects that he discovered while painting his sober pictures of peasants, whose skin tones could be made 'to stand out like lights' from their dingy surroundings. The image of lights is particularly apt when applied to the group of star-like daisies whose placement enhances the radiant effect he was after.

Van Gogh's hollyhocks were almost certainly inspired by the cottage garden pictures of Ernest Quost, a painter of 'magnificent and perfect hollyhocks' whom van Gogh deferred to as 'Père Quost', although he was only nine years older than van Gogh. Quost had first studied plants for his job as a decorator at Sèvres Porcelain Manufactory, and his close knowledge of them is evident in his paintings of flowers growing naturally in country gardens. His colours are light and fresh and van Gogh clearly considered him as much a colourist as the Impressionists.

37

MAJOLICA JAR WITH BRANCHES OF OLEANDER

1888. Oil, 60 × 73 cm (23³/₈ × 28³/₄ in)

Metropolitan Museum of Art, New York, F593 JH1566

'One of these days I hope to make a study of oleanders,' van Gogh wrote to Theo from Arles in August 1888 (Letter 524). His house overlooked a public garden where earlier he had painted summery impressions of oleander bushes. But he was now after a more complete statement that combined the clarity of Japanese drawing with the simplicity Manet achieved in painting peonies 'as free in the open air and as much a flower as anything could be, and yet painted in a perfectly solid impasto' (Letter 527, August 1888).

The oleander, so characteristic of the region, was yet another echo of the exotic Land of the Rising Sun as evoked by Pierre Loti in his romance *Madame Chrysanthème*. Van Gogh was clearly seduced by the flower's associations: 'The oleander – ah! that speaks of love and is beautiful like the Lesbos of Puvis de Chavannes, with women on the seashore' (Letter 587, April 1889). He even thought of planting two oleanders in tubs outside the front door of his Yellow House, and that thought may have guided his emotive choice of pink and green with a singing yellow for the painting illustrated here. The still life becomes a metaphor for a new, enhanced way of being in the South, for prominently positioned in the foreground is a copy of Zola's novel of 1884, *La Joie de vivre*. His earlier depiction of this book in a painting made in Nuenen a year after publication, placed it, significantly, beside the rejected authority of his father's Bible.

38

THISTLES ALONG THE ROAD

1888. Pencil, pen and brown ink, 24.5 × 32 cm (9⁷/₈ × 12⁵/₈ in)

National Museum Vincent van Gogh, Amsterdam,
F1466 JH1552

39

BLOSSOMING CHESTNUT BRANCHES (detail)

1890. Oil, 72 × 91 cm (28³/₈ × 35⁷/₈ in)

Foundation E.G. Bührle Collection, Zurich,
F820 JH2010

'Essentially the colour is exquisite here. When the green leaves are fresh, it is a rich green, the like of which we seldom see in the North, quiet. When it gets scorched and dusty, it does not lose its beauty,' van Gogh wrote of Arles (Letter W4, to Wil, June 1888). And in mid-August, ecstatic with the sun and heat, he reported: 'I have two studies of thistles in a vague field, thistles white with the fine dust of the road' (Letter 522, August 1888). And later: 'I am working on another study of dusty thistles, with an innumerable swarm of white and yellow butterflies.' (Letter 526, August 1888)

He also treated the subject in the independent drawing illustrated here in which the flat surface is made to pulsate with an inventive vocabulary of dashes, dots and flourishes. The crisply realized repertory of marks which van Gogh perfected in his pen and ink drawings was less easily accomplished in paint on account of the mistral. This troublesome wind gave all his attempts a 'haggard' look, van Gogh lamented, and made it 'very hard to get one's brushwork firm and interwoven with feeling, like a piece of music played with emotion' (Letter 543, September, 1888).

Unhampered by strong wind in Auvers, his painting *Blossoming Chestnut Branches* seems admirably to fulfil that aspiration. Its design is carefully controlled and integrated and it displays van Gogh's distinctive powers of conveying the sensation of flowers seen in the open air.

40

BOWL OF SUNFLOWERS, ROSES AND OTHER
FLOWERS (detail)

1886. Oil, 50 × 61 cm (19⅜ × 24 in)
Städtische Kunsthalle, Mannheim, F250 JH1166

The combination here of sunflowers, their first appearance in van Gogh's work, and pink cabbagy roses is highly idiosyncratic and scarcely a flower arranger's choice, but it clearly offered scope for an unusual exercise in colour gymnastics. The composition was probably the last of a group of four painted in the same ceramic vase, among them *Vase with Peonies and Roses* (Pl. 19). The variety of flowers and their casual placing in the container echoes the naturalistic treatment of other contemporary paintings, most obviously the *Still Life with Flowers* by Fantin-Latour of 1877, which Vincent and his brother Theo owned. Van Gogh's rendering with vigorous impasto brushstrokes is less particularized than Fantin-Latour's. He concentrates on establishing an overall harmony based on a dominant contrast of red and green and working out a counterpoint by means of repetitions and echoes. His painterly method of playing around with colours on the surface of the canvas, rather than creating an illusion of fore- and background, provoked a note of critical exasperation in a letter from Andries Bonger to his future brother-in-law, Theo: 'The flower-pieces are most gay and colourful as a whole; but some pictures are flat, a thing I am unable to convince him of. He persists in replying, But I wanted to introduce this or that colour contrast. As if I gave a damn about what he *wanted* to do!' The luscious bravura handling of paint in this still life should be compared to *Blossoming Chestnut Branches* (Pl. 39), a canvas done just four years later in 1890, to appreciate the direction in which van Gogh's experiments were leading him. His vision for the development of his painting had been realized – 'painting as it now promises to become more subtle – more like music and less like sculpture – and above all it promises *colour*' (Letter 528, August 1888).

41

FRITILLARIAS IN A COPPER VASE

1887. Oil, 73.5 × 60.5 cm (29¹/₈ × 24 in)

Musée d'Orsay, Paris, F213 JH1247

Painting in Paris in 1887, van Gogh has taken characteristic liberties with the flowers illustrated here, exaggerating movement and colour contrasts in search of a lively composition. His close friendship with the neo-Impressionist Paul Signac is evident in the strong blue/violet dotted ground, which provides a vibrating atmospheric surround to the fritillarias' flamboyant orange bells and their gleaming container. Van Gogh's own use of pointillism was restricted to the backgrounds of his still lifes, which always retained a solid, tangible reality (*see* Pl. 8). Replying no doubt to questions from Wil, van Gogh tried to explain to her something of what he was about:

'Cornflowers and white chrysanthemums and a certain number of marigolds – see here a motif in blue and orange.

Heliotrope and yellow roses – motif in lilac and yellow.

Poppies or red geraniums in vigorously green leaves – motif in red and green.

These are fundamentals, which one may subdivide further, and elaborate, but quite enough to show you without the help of a picture that there are colours which cause each other to shine brilliantly, which form a *couple*, which complete each other like man and woman.

Explaining the whole theory to you would involve quite a lot of writing, yet it might be done. Colourings, wallpapers and whatnot could be made much prettier by paying attention to the laws of colours.' (Letter W4, June/July 1888)

The floral backgrounds to his portraits effect this idea, but he also envisaged more elaborate and unconventional schemes of interior decoration: groupings of seven or nine canvases in which sunflowers like torches would illuminate his portraits of Augustine Roulin (*see* Pl. 12). And some years later he wrote to Theo from Auvers that he had noticed that a portrait of Dr Gachet's daughter went very well with a horizontal picture of wheat, adding, 'but we are still far from the time when people will understand the curious relation between one fragment of nature and another, which all the same explain each other and enhance each other' (Letter 645, June 1890).

42

FLOWERING ROSEBUSHES

1889. Oil, 33 × 42 cm (13 × 16¹/₂ in)

National Museum of Western Art, Tokyo, F580 JH1679

'I still can find no better definition of the word art than this, *L'art c'est l'homme a jouté à la nature* [art is man added to nature] – nature, reality, truth, but with a significance, a conception, a character, which the artist brings out in it, and to which he gives expression, *qu'il dégage*, which he disentangles, sets free and interprets.' (Letter 130, June 1879)
'If we study Japanese art, we see a man who is undoubtedly wise, philosophic and intelligent, who spends his time doing what? In studying the distance between the earth and moon? No. In studying Bismarck's policy? No. He studies a single blade of grass. But this blade of grass leads him to draw every plant and then the seasons, the wide aspects of the countryside, then animals, then the human figure. So he passes his life, and life is too short to do the whole.
Come now, isn't it almost a true religion which these simple Japanese teach us, who live in nature as though they themselves were flowers?
And you cannot study Japanese art, it seems to me, without becoming much gayer and happier, and we must return to nature in spite of our education and our work in a world of convention.' (Letter 542, September 1888)

FURTHER READING

The Complete Letters of Vincent van Gogh, 3 vols. Introduction by V. W. VAN BONGER; preface and memoir by J. VAN GOGH-BONGER. London and New York, 1958
Van Gogh à Paris, exhibition catalogue, Musée d'Orsay, by B. WELSH-OVCHAROV *et al* (in French), Paris, 1988
B. BERNARD (ed.), *Vincent by Himself: A selection of his paintings and drawings together with extracts from his letters*, London, 1985
D. COOPER *Drawings and Watercolours: A Selection of 32 Plates in Colour*, New York, 1955
V.W. VAN GOGH (ed.), *Vincent in the Borinage and Etten; Vincent at the Hague and Drenthe; Vincent at Nuenen; Vincent in Paris; Vincent at Arles; Vincent at Saint-Rémy; Vincent at Auvers-sur-Oise*, seven introductory booklets, National Museum Vincent van Gogh, Amsterdam, 1974-7
A.M. HAMMACHER and R. HAMMACHER, *Van Gogh: A Documentary Biography*, London, 1982

J. HULSKER, *The Complete van Gogh: Paintings, Drawings, Sketches*, Oxford and New York, 1980
M. MCQUILLAN, *Van Gogh*, London, 1989
R. PICKVANCE, *Van Gogh in Saint-Rémy and Auvers*, exhibition catalogue, The Metropolitan Museum of Art, New York, 1986
R. PICKVANCE, *Van Gogh in Arles*, exhibition catalogue, The Metropolitan Museum of Art, New York, 1984
G. POLLOCK and F. ORTON, *Vincent van Gogh: Artist of his Time*, Oxford and New York, 1978
J. REWALD, *Post-Impressionism: From van Gogh to Gauguin*, 3rd rev. edn., New York and London, 1978
M.W. ROSKILL, *Van Gogh, Gauguin and the Impressionist Circle*, New York, 1970
M. SCHAPIRO, *Vincent van Gogh*, New York, 1950
M. TRABAULT, *Vincent van Gogh*, New York, 1969

PHOTOGRAPHIC ACKNOWLEDGEMENTS

The publishers wish to thank all museums, galleries and others who have contributed towards the reproductions in this book. Further acknowledgement is made to the following:

Vincent van Gogh Foundation/National Museum Vincent van Gogh, Amsterdam: endpapers, 1, 2, 5, 7, 9, 10, 15, 16, 17, 21, 29, 32, 33, 34, 38; © Wadsworth Atheneum, Hartford, Connecticut.

Bequest of Anne Parrish Titzell: 30; reproduced by courtesy of the Trustees of the National Gallery, London: 6; Artothek, Munich (photograph): 27; © The Metropolitan Museum of Art, Rogers Fund, 1949: 28; Adele R. Levy, 1952 (photograph by Malcolm Varon): 31; Gift of Mr and Mrs John L. Loeb, 1962: 37; Sotheby's, New York (photograph): 14; Giraudon, Paris: 25, 41; Statens Konstmuseer, Stockholm (photograph): 24; The National Museum of Western Art, Tokyo, Matsuzaka Collection: 42.

INDEX

Figure in italic refer to plate numbers and their captions

Angelus, The (Millet) 13
Antwerp 16, 19, *36*
Arles, Provence 10, 19, 22, *17, 21, 23, 24, 27, 37, 39*)
Arums (endpapers)
Augustine Roulin (La Berceuse) 27, *41*; Pl. 12
Auvers *16, 23, 24, 25, 32, 39, 41*

Bernard, Émile 20, *13, 27*
Bing, Siegfried 19
Blossoming Almond Branch in a Glass 13; Pl. 1
Blossoming Branches Pl. 15
Blossoming Chestnut Branches 40; Pl. 39
Blossoming Pear Tree 14; Pl. 21
Bodmer, Karl *32*
Bonger, Andries *40*
Borinage 13
Bowl of Sunflowers, Roses and Other Flowers Pl. 40
Brabant 10
Branches of Almond Tree in Blossom Pl. 2
Branches of Flowering Acacia Pl. 24
Branches with Wild Roses Pl. 33
Breton, Jules *31*

Cézanne, Paul *25, 31*
Constable, John 12
Courbet, Gustave *19*

Death's-Head Moth on an Arum Pl. 16
Degas, Edgar *34*
Delacroix, Eugène 17, 19, *19, 34*

Fantin-Latour, Henri *19, 40*
Field of Grass with Dandelions and Tree Trunks Pl. 18
Fields with Poppies Pl. 26
Flowering Rose Bushes Pl. 42
Four Cut Sunflowers, One Upside Down Pl. 4
Fourteen Sunflowers in a Vase Pl. 6
Fritillarias in a Copper Vase Pl. 41

Gachet, Dr Paul-Ferdinand *23, 25*
Gainsborough, Thomas 16
Garden with Flowers 22; Pl. 35
Garden with Sunflowers 27; Pl. 9
Gauguin, Paul 9, *27*; Pl. 5
Goupil & Co. 12
Graphic, The 13

Hals, Frans 16, 17, *34*
Heine, Heinrich 12

Irises Pl. 14
Irises Pl. 22
Isaäcson, J.J. *31*

Japanese Vase with Roses and Anemones Pl. 25
Joie de Vivre, La (Zola) *37*
Jug with Red and White Carnations Pl. 20

Livens, Horace Mann *19, 30, 36*
London 12
Loti, Pierre *32, 37*

Madame Chrysanthème (Loti) *32, 37*
Majolica Jar with Branches of Oleander Pl. 37
Manet, Edouard *37*

Maris, (Matthijs) Thijs 12
Mauve, Anton 13, 15, 16, *13*
Mes Haines (Zola) 9
Millet, Jean-François 13, *31*
Mirbeau, Octave 24
Monet, Claude 19, *26, 34*
Monticelli, Adolphe 22, *18*

Nuenen *24, 34, 37*

Orchard with Blossoming Plum Trees Pl. 11

Paris 19, *27, 30, 41*
Pink Peach Trees Pl. 13
Pink Roses Pl. 23
Potato Eaters, The 11

Quost, Ernest *27, 36*

Rembrandt, Harmensz van Rijn 16
Renoir, Pierre-Auguste 19, *23, 34*
Rubens, Peter Paul 17, *19, 34*
Ruysdael, Jacob van 12, 16

Saint-Rémy, Provence 22, *16, 17, 18, 22, 23, 26, 31*
Signac, Paul *41*
Sisley, Alfred *34*
Sower, The 17
Still Life with Flowers (Fantin-Latour) *19, 40*
Streatham Common 12

Thistles along the Road Pl. 38
Twelve Sunflowers in a Vase Pl. 27
Two Cut Sunflowers, One Upside Down 27; Pl. 28

Van Gogh Painting Sunflowers (Gauguin) Pl. 5
van Gogh, Theodorus (Theo) 9, 15, *20, 21, 40*
van Gogh, Wilhelmina (Wil) *35, 39, 41*
Vase with Daisies and Anemones Pl. 8
Vase with Fourteen Sunflowers 27; Pl. 29
Vase with Gladioli Pl. 34
Vase with Hollyhocks Pl. 3
Vase with Peonies and Roses 40; Pl. 19
Vase with Pink Roses Pl. 10
Vase with Poppies Pl. 30
Vase with Poppies, Daisies, Cornflowers and Peonies 30; Pl. 36
Vase with Violet Irises against a Pink Background 17; Pl. 31
Vase with Violet Irises against a Yellow Background Pl. 17
Velázquez, Diego de *34*
Veronese, Paolo *34*

Wild Roses with a Beetle Pl. 32

Zola, Émile 9, 24, *14, 31, 41*
Zundert 10